B.C.
The Sun Comes Up
The Sun Goes Down

by

JOHNNY HART

FAWCETT GOLD MEDAL • NEW YORK

B.C. THE SUN COMES UP, THE SUN GOES DOWN

© 1973, 1974 Field Enterprises, Inc.
© 1979 Field Enterprises, Inc.

Published by Fawcett Gold Medal Books, a unit of
CBS Publications, the Consumer Publishing Division
of CBS Inc., by special arrangement with
Field Newspaper Syndicate.

ISBN: 0-449-14205-1

Printed in the United States of America

10   9   8   7   6   5   4   3   2   1

B.C.

A humble servant to
naivety. A most pleasant
encounter for those
who dislike encounters.

CURLS

The master of
sarcastic wit.

WILEY

A poet with an aversion
to water in any form and
an adherence to sports
in any shape.

PETER

A self-styled genius.
The world's first
philosophical failure...
and a mogul of forced
enterprise.

THOR

The inventor of the
wheel and the comb. A
self-proclaimed ladies'
man. And an artist.

GROG

A caveman's caveman.
A teddy bear for the
"macho."

CLUMSY CARP

A friendly, unassuming, myopic maladroit. An assiduous student of ichthyology. One who always leaves his best foot backward.

THE FAT BROAD

A ubiquitous "straight-person" with an unswerving devotion to the domination of men.

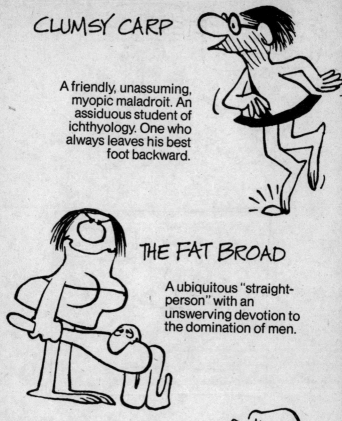

THE CUTE CHICK

A sex object in a world that had not yet discovered objectivity.

THOR: THE FIRST MAN TO INVENT A FORM OF TRANSPORTATION PROPELLED BY A JACKASS.

10.12

HOW CAN YOU WAKE UP FEELING SO GOOD IN THE MORNING?.....

1013

YOU'D FEEL GOOD TOO IF YOU HAD FIVE THOUSAND CRICKETS IN YOUR CAVE ALL NIGHT,..... SCREAMING "CHEER-UP!"

10·15

THE "MULTIFINNED BLOWFISH!"

10.19

SCHLOOP

.... THE MULTIFINNED SUCKFISH?.....

10-30

11-5

11·21

11-22

11-24

11·26

11·29

11-30

FOR 12 YEARS NOW HE'S HAD HIS HEAD STUCK IN THAT STUPID CREEK! ...WHAT DOES HE EXPECT TO PROVE?

BEATS ME.

......BALDNESS BY EROSION?

LOOK, LOOK, SEE Dick
don his shoulder pads,

SEE him slip into his
Hip pads,

12·11

SEE Dick adjust his
Helmet and mouthpiece.

Dick is going to a
Peace rally.

LOOK, see Dick take Jane
to a classy restaurant.

SEE Dick impress Jane by slipping
the maitred'a dime.

12·12

See Dick and Jane dining
in the meat locker.

hart

LOOK, LOOK. SEE Jane fight for equal-opportunity employment.

12·13

Oh, LOOK, SEE Jane win her case.

See Jane scraping the barnacles off the Queen Elizabeth.

EEYOWIEE

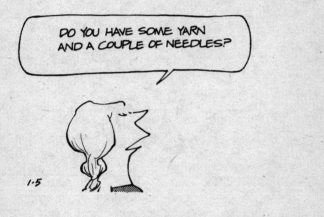

1·5

1-8

1-17

1·26

2·1

the fine line between thinking about doing it and doing it without thinking.

2·1

29

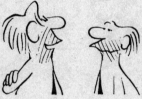

2·14

2-15

2-21

2·27

2·28

3.4

3·5

3·7

TWANG

3-13

3·14

WHAT'S IT WORTH TO YOU TO DOUBLE YOUR BUSINESS?

3·2(

IF YOU CAN DOUBLE MY BUSINESS, I'LL CUT YOU IN AS A PARTNER.

THERE.

3·21

3·23

3-25

3-26

3-28

3-29

4·1

4·2

4.4

48

4·10

4·11

4·12

4.13

4-22

4-24

FAWCETT GOLD MEDAL BOOKS
in the B.C. series by Johnny Hart include: